Great American Presidents

John F. Kennedy

GREAT AMERICAN PRESIDENTS

JOHN ADAMS

JOHN QUINCY ADAMS

JIMMY CARTER

THOMAS JEFFERSON

JOHN F. KENNEDY

ABRAHAM LINCOLN

RONALD REAGAN

FRANKLIN DELANO ROOSEVELT

THEODORE ROOSEVELT

HARRY S. TRUMAN

GEORGE WASHINGTON

WOODROW WILSON

GREAT AMERICAN PRESIDENTS

JOHN F. KENNEDY

SUSAN MUADDI DARRAJ

FOREWORD BY
WALTER CRONKITE

Philadelphia

CHELSEA HOUSE PUBLISHERS

VP, NEW PRODUCT DEVELOPMENT Sally Cheney
DIRECTOR OF PRODUCTION Kim Shinners
CREATIVE MANAGER Takeshi Takahashi
MANUFACTURING MANAGER Diann Grasse

STAFF FOR JOHN F. KENNEDY

ASSOCIATE EDITOR Kate Sullivan
PRODUCTION ASSISTANT Megan Emery
ASSISTANT PHOTO EDITOR Noelle Nardone
SERIES DESIGNER Keith Trego
COVER DESIGNER Keith Trego
LAYOUT 21st Century Publishing and Communications, Inc.

A Haights Cross Communications Company

www.chelseahouse.com

First Printing

1 3 5 7 9 8 6 4 2

Library of Congress Cataloging-in-Publication Data

Darraj, Susan Muaddi.
John F. Kennedy / Susan Muaddi Darraj.
p. cm. -- (Great American presidents)
Summary: A biography of the president who saw America through the Cuban Missile Crisis, established the Peace Corps, and was assasinated during his first term. Includes bibliographical references and index.
ISBN 0-7910-7600-8 -- ISBN 0-7910-7786-1 (pbk.)
1. Kennedy, John F. (John Fitzgerald), 1917-1963--Juvenile literature. 2. Presidents--United States--Biography--Juvenile literature. [1. Kennedy, John F. (John Fitzgerald), 1917-1963. 2. Presidents.] I. Title. II. Series.
E842.Z9D37 2003
973.922'092--dc22

2003014056

TABLE OF CONTENTS

FOREWORD

WALTER CRONKITE

A candle can defy the darkness. It need not have the power of a great searchlight to be a welcome break from the gloom of night. So it goes in the assessment of leadership. He who lights the candle may not have the skill or imagination to turn the light that flickers for a moment into a perpetual glow, but history will assign credit to the degree it is due.

Some of our great American presidents may have had a single moment that bridged the chasm between the ordinary and the exceptional. Others may have assured their lofty place in our history through the sum total of their accomplishments.

When asked who were our greatest presidents, we cannot fail to open our list with the Founding Fathers who put together this nation and nursed it through the difficult years of its infancy. George Washington, John Adams, Thomas Jefferson, and James Madison took the high principles of the revolution against British tyranny and turned the concept of democracy into a nation that became the beacon of hope to oppressed peoples around the globe.

Almost invariably we add to that list our wartime presidents—Abraham Lincoln, perhaps Woodrow Wilson, and certainly Franklin Delano Roosevelt.

Nonetheless there is a thread of irony that runs through the inclusion of the names of those wartime presidents: In many aspects their leadership was enhanced by the fact that, without objection from the people, they assumed extraordinary powers to pursue victory over the nation's enemies (or, in the case of Lincoln, the Southern states).

The complexities of the democratic procedures by which the United States Constitution deliberately tried to withhold unchecked power from the presidency encumbered the presidents who needed their hands freed of the entangling bureaucracy that is the federal government.

Much of our history is written far after the events themselves took place. History may be amended by a much later generation seeking a precedent to justify an action considered necessary at the latter time. The history, in a sense, becomes what later generations interpret it to be.

President Jefferson in 1803 negotiated the purchase of vast lands in the south and west of North America from the French. The deal became knows as the Louisiana Purchase. A century and a half later, to justify seizing the nation's steel mills that were being shut down by a labor strike, President Truman cited the Louisiana Purchase as a case when the president in a major matter ignored Congress and acted almost solely on his own authority.

The case went to the Supreme Court, which overturned Truman six to three. The chief justice, Fred Vinson, was one of the three justices who supported the president. Many historians, however, agreed with the court's majority, pointing out that Jefferson scarcely acted alone: Members of Congress were in the forefront of the agitation to consummate the Louisiana Purchase and Congress voted to fund it.

With more than two centuries of history and precedent now behind us, the Constitution is still found to be flexible when honest and sincere individuals support their own causes with quite different readings of it. These are the questions that end up for interpretation by the Supreme Court.

As late as the early years of the twenty-first century, perhaps the most fateful decision any president ever can make—to commit the nation to war—was again debated and precedent ignored. The Constitution says that only the Congress has the authority to declare war. Yet the Congress, with the objection of few members, ignored this Constitutional provision and voted to give President George W. Bush the right to take the United States to war whenever and under whatever conditions he decided.

Thus a president's place in history may well be determined by how much power he seizes or is granted in re-interpreting and circumventing the remarkable document that is the Constitution. Although the Founding Fathers thought they had spelled out the president's authority in their clear division of powers between the branches of the executive, the legislative and the judiciary, their wisdom has been challenged frequently by ensuing generations. The need and the demand for change is dictated by the march of events, the vast alterations in society, the global condition beyond our influence, and the progress of technology far beyond the imaginations of any of the generations which preceded them.

The extent to which the powers of the presidency will be enhanced and utilized by the chief executives to come in large degree will depend, as they have throughout our history, on the character of the presidents themselves. The limitations on those powers, in turn, will depend on the strength and will of those other two legs of the three-legged stool of American government—the legislative and the judiciary.

And as long as this nation remains a democracy, the final say will rest with an educated electorate in perpetual exercise of its constitutional rights to free speech and a free and alert press.

1

Son of American Royalty

THE KENNEDY ESTATE in perpetually sunny Palm Beach, Florida, was a favorite of the entire family. Bought in the early 1930s by Joseph P. Kennedy, the patriarch of the Kennedy clan, to be the family's winter home, the mansion featured Spanish-style red tiles and gleaming white stucco walls. For Kennedy's second-eldest son, John—nicknamed "Jack"—the Palm Beach mansion was also an ideal getaway, perfect for relaxation and time away from a grueling public life. Soon after the 1960 presidential election, in which Jack defeated Richard Nixon, an older and more seasoned candidate, he retreated to Palm Beach during the Christmas and New Year holidays to work on his inaugural address.

John F. Kennedy, pictured here in his Senate office, became president in 1961, during a tumultuous time in the United States. He won the presidential election against Richard Nixon by one of the smallest margins in the history of the presidency: 118,550 votes.

The speech had to be a gem. After all, the election had been one of the closest in American history, with Jack earning only 118,550 more votes than Nixon. With the country split almost down the middle, the speech had to both energize his supporters and reassure his opponents.

It also had to relieve the anxiety of all Americans. World War II had come to a close in 1945 with the dropping of the atomic bomb on the Japanese cities of Hiroshima and Nagasaki. Americans were still suffering from the loss of lives and the unstable economy. Racial strife and fear of nuclear war terrified them. America's youth in particular sought a hopeful vision for the future. They wanted a president who would restore the nation and help them move forward. Kennedy had just barely been elected to be that leader.

Realizing the importance of the inaugural speech, Jack's circle of supporters offered encouragement; some even drafted the speech for him. They forgot, though, that this was one area in which the soon-to-be-president needed little—if any—help. Writing was one of his many talents—one that he especially loved. Christmas of 1960 and New Year's Day of 1961 were largely spent at a poolside table, where Jack clacked away on his portable typewriter, pausing frequently to consult his many pages of notes. He also reread copies of other famous speeches, such as Abraham Lincoln's Gettysburg Address, delivered during another moment when the country had been divided—the Civil War.

> *"Let the word go forth from this time and place, to friend and foe alike, that the torch has been passed to a new generation of Americans."*
>
> — John F. Kennedy, inaugural address

Concentrating on his speech during a family holiday was not an easy task, especially with a new baby in the house. John F. Kennedy Jr. had been born just three weeks after the election, and like all babies he demanded attention. Jack's daughter Caroline was a toddler who loved being with her father as much as her father loved being with her. This holiday, though, would not be a fun or relaxing one for Jack. His wife, Jacqueline, kept Caroline and baby

John indoors, allowing Jack to focus on one of the most important speeches of his career, to write the words that would electrify a whole generation of Americans.

THE AMERICAN DREAM

Many people would say that Jack Kennedy was destined for fame, but his family roots and his own childhood—filled with insecurity, ill health, and tragedy—could hardly be described as glamorous.

Both Jack's maternal great-grandparents, the Fitzgeralds, and his paternal great-grandparents, the Kennedys, fled Ireland during the potato famine of the 1840s, crossing the Atlantic Ocean on one of the many "coffin ships" that brought immigrants to the United States. These vessels earned their morbid nickname from the vast number of people who died of illness or malnutrition during the long, difficult voyage and the dank, cramped conditions onboard. Like many Catholic Irish immigrants, they settled in Boston, appreciating the safety of numbers in light of all the anti-Catholic and anti-Irish prejudice in the United States at the time. (It was not uncommon for businesses to advertise job openings and add that no Irish should apply.)

> *"I believe in an America where religious intolerance will someday end—where all men and all churches are treated as equal . . . where Catholics, Protestants, and Jews . . . will refrain from those attitudes of disdain and division which have so often marred their works in the past, and promote instead the American ideal of brotherhood."*
>
> — John F. Kennedy, in an address to the Greater Houston Ministerial Association, September 12, 1960

The descendants of the Kennedy and Fitzgerald immigrants were unafraid of hard work and were determined to live the American dream. Jack's paternal grandfather, Patrick Joseph Kennedy, opened his own saloon and soon became a local politician. His son, Joseph Patrick Kennedy, attended Harvard College, which, like most of the other elite universities in New England, was a stronghold of Protestantism and wealth. Because he was Catholic and of Irish descent, Joseph always felt excluded from certain social circles.

Later in his life, when he had risen to national political prominence, Joseph resented being called an "Irishman." "I was born in this country," he raged. "My children were born in this country. What the hell does someone have to do to become an American?" He spent his life trying to overcome the anti-Catholic prejudice that often put obstructions in his path, such as when he was "blackballed," or refused admittance, by an exclusive country club in 1922.

Soon after graduating from college, Joseph saved the bank at which he was employed from financial trouble. In return he was appointed president, and, at the age of 25, he was the youngest bank president in American history. After experiencing success in the stock market, he became a multimillionaire. His marriage to Rose Fitzgerald, the daughter of Boston's mayor, in October 1914 further elevated his already fast-rising social status.

Rose's father, John Francis Fitzgerald, affectionately called "Honey Fitz" because of his infamous sweet tooth,

Joseph and Rose Fitzgerald Kennedy were married in October 1914. Joseph was an educated man who often felt excluded from society because of his Irish background. Rose was the daughter of John "Honey" Fitzgerald, the mayor of Boston. She was intensely religious, a trait that she tried to instill in her children.

was the mayor of Boston and a popular politician. The people of Boston knew Honey Fitz as their charismatic leader, someone who could work long hours to run the city effectively as well as dance and sing Irish ballads long into the night. His exuberance and zest for life were legendary: At a local baseball game, he once saved the lives of several children by pushing them out of the way of a truck that had veered out of control. The children were unhurt, but the vehicle struck him, badly injuring his legs. A nervous crowd gathered around him as he lay in pain on the field, but he reassured them all by singing "Sweet Adeline" until medical help arrived.

Rose inherited almost none of her father's liveliness—indeed, she was a serious young woman who adhered to her Catholic faith and was deeply religious. Having spent her formative years in a convent school, she would apply the discipline she learned there later in life when she was raising Jack and his eight siblings, whom she escorted to Mass every morning and with whom she knelt down to pray every night.

A COMPETITIVE CHILDHOOD

Rose and Joseph doted on their first child, Joseph Patrick Jr., who embodied all his parents' hopes to make the Kennedy name famous. When Rose and Joseph had more money, they moved out of the city, purchasing a modest clapboard house at 83 Beals Street in Brookline, a suburb west of Boston.

Jack was born in the master bedroom of this house on May 29, 1917. His mother, always very organized, kept an index card on each of her children—nine in total—on which she wrote their birth dates, any illnesses, allergies, medications, and other essential information. Young Jack's card was soon filled with a list of all his medical problems,

The Kennedys had nine children, of which Jack (third from left) was the second-oldest son. He and his older brother, Joseph (second from right), were fiercely competitive during childhood and even in later years. Jack knew that his brother was the favorite son and that their parents' dreams rested with Joe Jr.

including "whooping cough, measles, [and] chicken pox," as well as scarlet fever, which he contracted when he was only two and a half years old.

In the early half of the century, scarlet fever—highly contagious and often fatal—was responsible for the deaths of many of its young victims. Jack was suspended between life and death for many days at the Boston City Hospital, which was already crowded with scarlet fever victims. His father remained by his side, praying fervently for his son's life to be spared. Jack did recover from his first encounter with death.

Jack's childhood is a laundry list of illnesses and health problems. His brother Robert (Bobby) claimed many years later, "When we were growing up together we used to laugh about the great risk a mosquito took in biting Jack Kennedy—with some of his blood the mosquito was almost sure to die."

Indeed, Jack suffered from bowel and stomach problems and would even contract malaria (which he controlled with medication) as a young man. There was also his back: His spine had never been very strong because the right side of his body was actually bigger than the left. His left shoulder hung slightly lower than his right shoulder, an abnormality that twisted his spine and made it vulnerable to injury.

Nevertheless, Jack was active in sports in school, playing for the football team and competing with the swim team. This rigorous schedule led to complications with his back. He endured several surgeries to ease the pain that often erupted, and at one point, doctors even inserted a steel plate in his back to reinforce his spine.

In general, Jack's childhood was filled with warmth and love. Rose Kennedy certainly had her hands full with her children, but she managed to maintain order. Lunch was served at 1:15 P.M. and dinner at 7:00 P.M.—tardiness was not tolerated. She and Joseph encouraged the children to learn and excel. An avid reader, Rose passed on her love of books to all her children, but especially to Jack. He enjoyed long car rides with his parents, during which Rose explained the significance of historical sites. At the dinner table, Joseph quizzed his children on current events. Because of their parents' relentless teaching, the Kennedy children were very well versed in politics, culture, history, and world affairs.

Life as a Kennedy son, however, was not quite as rosy as it appeared. Perhaps because of Rose and Joseph's intense pressure on Jack and his siblings, a powerful current of competitiveness ran through the Kennedy clan. Joe Jr., the oldest brother, was their father's favorite son—Jack understood this and felt it deeply. Because Joe was taller and physically stronger than Jack, the younger brother was conscious of living in Joe's shadow, certain that no matter how hard he worked, his father would always view his achievements with less enthusiasm than he viewed Joe's.

Because of his resentment of Joe's status as the eldest and favorite son, as well as his frequent illnesses, Jack enjoyed spending time alone lost in his books. His favorite stories were adventure stories, especially those about the mythic King Arthur and the Knights of the Round Table. History and current events also intrigued him, and when he began attending the Choate School, an elite preparatory school in Connecticut, in 1931, he was probably the only student to subscribe to *The New York Times.*

At Choate, he became ill so frequently—stomach pains, asthma, influenza, and other ailments—that he spent many days in the infirmary reading. For Jack, books represented an opportunity to escape from his physical pain, as well as from the fact that he was only an "average" student in terms of grades. Being average was a tragedy when he compared his grades to the superior ones of Joe, who also attended Choate.

His poor health, however, did not hinder Jack's social life. In fact, his personality blossomed when he was out of Joe's shadow, and his natural charisma attracted many schoolmates into his circle of friends. As the ringleader of the Muckers Club, a boisterous group of students who spent more time concocting pranks than studying, Jack became known as a chief mischief-maker at Choate and was once almost expelled for his behavior. Nevertheless, his intelligence and talent were undeniable: His schoolmates were aware that he practically devoured books and could answer many more questions on the popular radio quiz show *Information, Please* than they could. The bright star of his future was recognized by his classmates, who voted him "most likely to succeed" despite his academic rank of 64 in a class of 116 students.

THE DRUMS OF WAR

Joseph Kennedy Sr.'s star was also rising—and reaching heights that would affect the future of his entire family. In 1934, his financial savvy and success led to an appointment as the chairman of the newly formed Securities and Exchange Commission (SEC), the organization that regulates stocks, bonds, and other forms of investment that form the securities market in the United States. In 1938, President Franklin Delano Roosevelt appointed him ambassador to England—an important assignment that he knew would improve his sons' chances to become

Joseph Kennedy Sr. was appointed ambassador to England in 1938. At the time, Jack was enrolled in Harvard's Department of Government. In 1938, Joe Jr., Joe Sr., and Jack boarded the liner S.S. *Normandie* to travel to Britain. Jack accompanied his father in order to learn about government operation first-hand.

political leaders. With a foot in the political realm, Joseph was more determined than ever that Joe Jr. would become president of the United States. Because America had never before had a Catholic president, everything possible had to be done to improve Joe's odds.

Jack was in his sophomore year at Harvard when his father's assignment offered him an opportunity to travel to England. He had tried to break the family tradition of attending Harvard by enrolling at Princeton University in 1935. After all, his father had attended Harvard and his older brother was a student there at the time. After living in Joe Jr.'s shadow at Choate, Jack wanted to be at a school where his brother's seemingly perfect achievements would not eclipse his own. However, because of his health, Jack did not begin his studies at Princeton until the end of October, and further illnesses forced him to withdraw that December. In the fall of the following year, he enrolled and began his studies (one year late) in Harvard's newly established Department of Government. His first major attempt to make an independent decision had been thwarted by his health.

Jack met with eagerness his father's suggestion that he learn about government operations up-close by spending time in London. Harvard granted his request to spend the spring semester of his junior year abroad, despite his C average. Among the people he met during those critical few months were the future Queen Elizabeth and Eugenio Cardinal Pacelli, soon to be elected as Pope Pius XII. Joseph encouraged his son to cross the English Channel and spend time on the European continent on his own. Jack enjoyed those weeks touring France, Germany, Poland, Lithuania, the Soviet Union, and even the Middle East, where, on his last night in Jerusalem, he was awakened by the sounds of bomb explosions.

He returned to England in June but went back to the Continent, where he toured more sites and became enthralled by the history and culture of Europe despite the visible tension and expectations of war. On September 1, 1939, as he was returning to London, news came that

Germany's forces had invaded Poland. On September 3, Jack, his mother, his sister Kathleen, and Joe Jr. accompanied Joseph, the ambassador, to the British House of Commons to hear future prime minister Winston Churchill proclaim: "We are fighting to save the whole world from the pestilence of Nazi tyranny and in defence of all that is most sacred to man."

England was now at war with Germany and Adolf Hitler's Third Reich. World War II had begun, and the world would never be the same.

2

Eyewitness to History

ADOLF HITLER HAD been making Europe's leaders—as well as President Roosevelt—nervous for a long time. In October 1937, President Roosevelt warned that the hostility of Germany, Italy, and Japan threatened all civilized nations. Italy had invaded Ethiopia in 1935, Japan had launched a war against China in 1937, and Germany and Japan had withdrawn from the League of Nations, the organization that had been formed after World War I (and that later evolved into the United Nations).

Germany acted most aggressively of all: It seized control of Austria in March of 1938 and part of Czechoslovakia in September 1938. This last move was done with the permission of England and

France during a summit in Munich, at which the two allies hoped to avoid a war by appeasing Hitler. They promised not to attack Germany over Czechoslovakia if Hitler agreed to stop his attacks on neighboring nations. The German dictator would not be satisfied so easily.

When Hitler's forces seized the rest of Czechoslovakia in March 1939, England and France realized that Hitler planned to dominate all of Europe. This meant reducing England and France, the two strongest European nations, to an inferior status. Hitler used the ideologies of fascism—racism, rejection of democracy, and preference of force—to his advantage. Despite the terror he unleashed on the ethnic, religious, and social minorities that he controlled—such as Jews, gypsies, and Catholics—most Germans supported Hitler's goal of Germany becoming the most powerful nation in Europe.

When Hitler invaded Poland on September 1, 1939, the same day Jack Kennedy was flying back from the Continent to reunite with his family in London, World War II became a reality. As Jack sat in the House of Commons two days later listening to the British declaration of war, the fact that he was witnessing history deeply impressed him.

THE MAKING OF A WRITER

When Jack returned to Harvard a couple of weeks later, the task of choosing a topic for his senior honors thesis awaited him. A graduation requirement, the thesis was supposed to discuss an issue relevant to governmental

Jack, photographed here during his travels in the 1930s, spent much time touring Eastern and Western Europe and the Middle East. While in Europe, Jack met the future Queen Elizabeth II and future Pope Pius XII, then known as Eugenio Cardinal Pacelli, contacts that would serve him in his later political career.

affairs. Invigorated by his experiences in continental Europe and England, Jack, the C-average student, chose to explore why he thought England was unprepared for war with Germany. Most students chose "safe" topics—musings on ancient bills and past governmental controversies. Jack, however, tackled the most current of current events as the war raged across the Atlantic Ocean and Americans debated whether or not the United States should become involved.

Entitled "Appeasement at Munich," Jack's thesis described how England's government, specifically Prime Minister Neville Chamberlain, should have long ago recognized the threat Hitler and his regime posed to Europe. He criticized England and France for allowing Hitler to invade Czechoslovakia in 1938. The British Royal Air Forces, Jack claimed, were sorely lacking in preparation to effectively combat the German war machine. Finally, he asserted, England should have known that Hitler would not be satisfied with his defeat of Czechoslovakia and would make the inevitable move to conquer the rest of the Continent.

Although Jack's writing style was graceful, advanced, and intelligent, the content of "Appeasement at Munich" was entirely inaccurate. Germany had not caught England unprepared in the least. The island nation was ready for battle; it had been rearming and training for years, even while negotiating for peace.

The fact remains that Jack's thesis—approximately 30,000 words (twice the typical length for undergraduate theses), plus 350 footnotes—demonstrated exceptional writing talent for a 23-year-old.

Of course, Jack loved to write as much as he loved to read. Banging away at the typewriter allowed him to ponder questions, analyze information, and arrive at conclusions that resolved the issues he tackled. Jack had long been writing persuasive essays. At age 10, Jack decided that his 40-cent allowance was insufficient. When he asked for a raise, he was told that his father would have to be persuaded. With images of new purchases in his mind, Jack dedicated himself to this task. The result was "A Plea for a Raise, by Jack Kennedy. Dedicated to my father, Mr. J.P. Kennedy," a document that argued that the current 40 cents provided for the purchasing of "aeroplanes and other playthings of childhood, but now I am a scout and put away my childish things." As a scout, he needed more expensive items, such as "canteens and haversacks,"—but he noted that these costlier purchases "will last for years" and were worth the investment. Jack's efforts convinced his father to raise his allowance by 30 cents.

"When power leads man towards arrogance, poetry reminds him of his limitations. When power narrows the areas of man's concern, poetry reminds him of the richness and diversity of his existence. When power corrupts, poetry cleanses. For art establishes the basic human truth which must serve as the touchstone of our judgment."

— John F. Kennedy, address at Harvard University, 1956

Because Joe Jr. was slated to be the leader in the family, Jack nursed his dream of becoming a writer. He once told a reporter, "I would rather have the Pulitzer than be

President." Jack longed to be another Ernest Hemingway, the modern adventurer and writer who reported from war fronts all over the world and whose novels were devoured by his fans, including Jack.

George Gordon, Lord Byron, the dashing Romantic English poet of the late eighteenth and early nineteenth centuries, also fascinated Jack. The author of such classic poems as "She Walks in Beauty" and the epic *Don Juan*, Byron championed the cause of the oppressed all over the world—in fact, he died at the age of 36 fighting in the Greek war of independence. Perhaps the attraction for young Jack Kennedy was the fact that Byron excelled at many things—including the pursuit of women, poetry, politics, and a life of adventure—despite a physical ailment: a clubfoot. This deformity caused Byron to limp all his life, but he learned to live a full life in spite of it. To Jack, who suffered from what seemed like every conceivable illness known to the human race, Byron was a role model.

Jack's father recognized the remarkable intelligence of his second son. When Jack showed interest in having his thesis published as a book, Joseph helped him make the necessary connections. Arthur Krock, who had won the Pulitzer for his political writing in *The New York Times*, was a friend of Joseph, and he agreed to read Jack's manuscript. Enthusiastic about seeing the paper in book form, Krock

> *"If more politicians knew poetry, and more poets knew politics, I am convinced the world would be a little better place in which to live."*
>
> **— John F. Kennedy, address at Harvard University, 1956**

JOHN FITZGERALD KENNEDY

Born May 29, 1917, in Brookline, Massachusetts. Prepared at The Choate School. Home Address: 294 Pondfield Road, Bronxville, New York. Winthrop House. *Crimson* (2–4); Chairman Smoker Committee (1); St. Paul's Catholic Club (1–4). Football (1), Junior Varsity (2); Swimming (1), Squad (2). Golf (1). House Hockey (3, 4); House Swimming (2); House Softball (4). Hasty Pudding-Institute of 1770; Spee Club. Permanent Class Committee. Field of Concentration: Government. Intended Vocation: Law.

Jack's Harvard College yearbook photograph includes many of the young man's interests and reflects his focus on extracurricular interests. Jack wrote his thesis, a requirement for graduation from Harvard, about the political situation in Europe in 1939. Although the premise of the paper—that Germany had caught England off-guard when it invaded Poland in 1939—was generally inaccurate, the writing itself proved that Jack had talent.

suggested that the title be changed from "Appeasement in Munich" to "Why England Slept." This title recalled the phrase "while England slept," made popular as the title of a book by Winston Churchill, one of Jack's heroes. Because Jack argued that England had been slow in taking the German threat of war seriously, the new title was more than appropriate.

Copies of the book were printed rapidly and appeared on bookshelves while the topic was still current and people were anxiously following news of the war across the ocean. Even though its premise was essentially incorrect—England had indeed been prepared for Hitler's aggression—*Why England Slept* became a bestseller and transformed its 23-year-old author into someone to be taken seriously.

When Joe Jr. read Jack's book, he reportedly said to his father, "It represents a lot of work, but it does not prove anything." Some historians believe that the comment had more to do with the continuing competition between the brothers than with Joe's real feelings. Like his father, Joe Jr. believed that the United States should stay out of World War II. There was nothing to be gained by joining in the war against Hitler, because it was taking place in Europe—an ocean away—and would not affect the United States directly.

In *Why England Slept,* Jack opposed the isolationist view of his father and elder brother. It was inevitable, he believed, that the United States would enter the war. He was right.

3

THE HERO OF *PT-109*

ON DECEMBER 7, 1941, two months after Jack was accepted into the Naval Reserve, the Japanese air forces bombed Pearl Harbor, the United States base in Hawaii. More than 2,400 people died, and President Franklin D. Roosevelt declared December 7, 1941, as a day that would "live in infamy." He also announced that the nation would join England, France, and the other Allied Powers in war against the Axis powers: Germany, Japan, and Italy. As the nation prepared itself for the difficult road ahead, young men and women rushed to enlist in a war that had suddenly become personal.

Joe Jr. and Jack's desire to beat each other at everything was stronger than ever. Enlisting in the war was no different.

Joe Jr. enlisted in the Naval Reserve during World War II and spent most of that time in the Air Force. Not to be outdone, Jack enlisted in the Naval Reserve. Joe Jr. was killed in 1944 when his plane exploded while he was on a mission over England. The Kennedy parents' dreams thus fell to Jack to fulfill.

Joe Jr. had joined the Naval Reserve in the summer of 1941, attaining the rank of Seaman Second Class. His parents, who were isolationists and feared for their eldest son, on whom they had pinned all their hopes, were worried that he would be harmed. Joe's act only made Jack determined to do the same himself.

Jack's illnesses had taken a toll on his health: He failed the army and navy physical examinations and was deemed unfit to perform his duties. Other young men might have been happy for an excuse not to join the war, but Jack was furious. It was unacceptable that Joe Jr. would glean the glory of battle while Jack sat at home, ill and useless.

Being the son of a millionaire politician had its advantages, and Jack convinced his father to write to naval officials on his behalf. On August 5, 1941, Jack submitted to another physical examination at the Naval Reserve. The only physical defects, they noted, were three missing teeth. No mention was made of his weak, twisted back or of his long medical history. He was admitted to the Naval Reserve at a rank higher than his brother.

> *"I can imagine a no more rewarding career. And any man who may be asked in this century what he did to make his life worthwhile, I think can respond with a good deal of pride and satisfaction: 'I served in the United States Navy.'"*
>
> — John F. Kennedy, remarks at the United States Naval Academy, August 1, 1963

WAR HERO

One of the new technologies to emerge during World War II was the PT—a small, fast boat that was becoming more and more popular in the war. PTs were especially useful in fighting the Japanese in the southern Pacific Ocean because they could dart quickly around the many islands that dotted the sea.

Jack used his father's influence once again to gain

command of one of these ships. Having spent his summers in Palm Beach sailing with Joe Jr., he could handle a boat skillfully. Joseph persuaded the leader of a squadron of PT boats to give his son command of one. What Jack didn't know was that Joseph added, "See that he's sent someplace that isn't too deadly."

Those words failed to protect Jack from the harshness of the war.

Now a naval lieutenant, he was assigned to *PT-109*, an 80-foot boat powered by three engines. It had already seen battle and was in bad state. Jack worked valiantly to gather a team to man it and ready it for action.

A squadron of PTs, including Jack's, was assigned to monitor the Blackett Strait near the Russell Islands in the South Pacific. Their mission was to block Japanese warships, a fleet known as the Tokyo Express, which carried weapons and military arms across the strait and delivered them to other Japanese bases and forts.

On the night of August 1, 1943, *PT-109* crawled forward in the waters, patrolling the waterway. It moved slowly to avoid making a lot of noise and to remain hidden from the Japanese floatplanes buzzing overhead and the destroyers sailing nearby. Jack stood in the cockpit, peering into the night's darkness, relying on sight and sound to detect any danger because the small boat lacked radar capability.

What he did not know was that the Tokyo Express had already eluded other patrol PT boats and was moving rapidly down the strait.

At nearly 2:30 in the morning, one of Jack's crewmen yelled out, "Ship at two o'clock!" Everyone aboard *PT-109* scrambled to attention, and Jack ordered, "Full power!" desperately trying to avoid a collision with the massive vessels.

It was too late. The *Amagiri,* a Japanese destroyer, suddenly appeared out of the darkness, ripping into *PT-109* and tearing off a large section of its starboard (right) side. The fuel tanks ruptured, pouring 2,000 gallons of fuel into the sea. Jack ordered everyone to jump overboard, and after ripping up his codebook, leapt over himself. The ship exploded, the flames eating away at the shattered vessel.

The Americans bobbed in the icy waters, surrounded by the broken shards of their boat and a ring of fire. Most of the flames, however, were pulled away by the *Amagiri*'s wake as it continued up the strait, leaving Jack and his crew to drown in the sea.

His back aching, Jack swam to each man, taking a head count and assessing the situation. He and eight survivors hoisted themselves onto the half of *PT-109* that was still afloat. Then, hearing cries for help, Jack spotted two more men in the water. Pulling off his boots, Jack dove in again, swam over, and helped them back to the boat. Two men were still missing, having died in the collision. There was a flare gun he could fire to signal for help, but Jack knew it could bring back the Japanese destroyer or alert the Japanese stationed on nearby islands. That would be the end of them all.

Jack was the captain of *PT-109,* a specialized ship stationed in the South Pacific. He became a decorated war hero when a Japanese ship ripped through *PT-109,* causing it to explode. Jack (center, pictured with three crewmen) saved the lives of most of his crew.

When daybreak arrived, the crew swam through shark-infested waters toward Plum Pudding Island, three and a half miles away. Each man grasped an edge of a long piece of timber and set out as a unit. One crewman's hands had been so severely burned that he couldn't hold the timber like the rest. Jack clamped a strap of the crewman's life jacket between his teeth and pulled him along for the entire four hours it took to reach the tiny island. Finding no food or fresh water there, the next day Jack and the crew swam to Olasana Island, which was rich in coconut trees. Once again, Jack towed the injured crewman, this time on his back, refusing to leave him behind.

Throughout the ordeal, Jack maintained his composure. Despite a high fever, exhaustion, and severe back pain, Jack set an example of fearlessness for his men. Doctors would later determine that he had contracted malaria. He swam out into the sea countless times trying to flag down another PT boat, but his efforts were futile. On August 5, while his men waited on Olasana, he and another crewman swam to yet another island, where they encountered two natives. (Island natives were technically a neutral party in the war, but they often helped the Allies against the Japanese.) They hurried away in their canoe, but Jack saw them again the next day upon returning to his crew on Olasana.

The men, named Biuku Gasa and Eroni Kumana, agreed to help the stranded Americans. Jack carved a message into a still-green coconut: *Nauro Island Native Knows Posit He Can Pilot 11 Alive Need Small Boat Kennedy.* He gave the coconut and the knife to the men to scratch out the message in case they were discovered by the Japanese.

On August 7, a group of natives canoed back, carrying food for the Americans and a request from a British naval commander stationed nearby that Jack return on the canoe. Lying in the bottom of the canoe hidden by palm fronds, Jack was safely escorted by the natives past the Japanese forces to the British. "Hello," he said to the British officer, with a broad smile on his lips. "I'm Kennedy."

He was also a hero. He was eventually recognized with the Navy and Marine Corps Medal and cited for "extremely heroic conduct as Commanding Officer of Motor Torpedo Boat 109."

> *"It was absolutely involuntary. They sank my boat."*
>
> — John F. Kennedy, on being asked about becoming a war hero

Jack was a hero who recognized the pain that accompanied the glory of battle. He openly mourned the two men who had been killed: Wishing the other PT boats in the area had spotted him, he said, "If only they'd come over to help me, maybe I might have been able to save those other two."

THE BURDEN OF THE ELDEST

Although Jack was safe after his ordeal at sea, the devastation of the war years was not quite over for the Kennedys. A few months after Jack was decorated as a hero, the Kennedys received tragic news at their home in Hyannis Port, Massachusetts: While flying a bombing mission in Europe, Joe Jr.'s plane had exploded, killing the star Kennedy son.

The family was devastated, especially Jack, who understood that Joe Jr. had volunteered for the mission, known to be a dangerous one, even though he had already satisfied his commitments to the Navy. It seemed probable that in the wake of Jack's fame in the *PT-109* incident, Joe Jr. had wanted to claim some battle glory for himself.

Jack also realized that Joe Jr.'s death now meant that the burden of being the eldest—fulfilling all his father's

For his heroic actions in rescuing his men from the *PT-109* explosion, Jack was awarded the Navy and Marine Corps Medal. He always regretted that he had not been able to save the lives of the two lost crewmen.

hopes and ambitions—would soon be placed on his shoulders. He confided in a friend, "I'm shadowboxing a match the shadow is always going to win."

He vented his sadness in writing, compiling essays written by family and friends about his elder brother into a book, *As We Remember Joe.* He also briefly pursued a journalism career. As Jack had suspected, Joseph was intent on getting his second son into a position of national prominence, so he supported the idea of Jack becoming a journalist. It would get his name into the papers and known to the American public, Joseph reasoned, so he spoke with his friend William Randolph Hearst, a major newspaper publisher, to help Jack land choice writing assignments.

One of those assignments was to report on the April 25, 1945 conference in San Francisco that would lay the foundation for the United Nations. Once again, Jack was a direct witness to the making of history.

He knew, though, that the career of a writer would not last more than a few months. Sadly, he told a friend, “I can’t just do what I like, and I’m sure now that Joe is dead, I’m going into politics.”

4

Congressman Kennedy

ON AUGUST 6, 1945, President Harry Truman authorized the dropping of the atomic bomb on the Japanese city of Hiroshima, killing over 80,000 people. Three days later, on August 9, a second bomb was dropped on Nagasaki. Almost a week later, the Japanese surrendered and World War II was over.

The war had scarred the Kennedys, as it had most American families. Still, the Kennedy dream persisted. Just as Jack had predicted, he now carried all his parents' hopes, especially the biggest—to bring the Kennedy name into the Oval Office.

The first logical step was to gain political experience. On April 25, 1946, almost a year after the end of World War II,

Jack began his political experience when he ran for the United States Congress in 1946. He cast a vote—presumably for himself—and won the election by one of the biggest landslides in congressional history. Pictured with him at the Democratic primary are his maternal grandparents, the Fitzgeralds.

Jack announced his plan to run for a seat in the House of Representatives for the Eleventh Congressional District of Massachusetts. One of ten candidates seeking the position, he decided to rely on the strategies of his beloved grandfather, Honey Fitz, to campaign among Bostonians. His grandfather, after all, had been mayor of Boston after being a congressman himself. "You are my namesake," Honey Fitz told Jack once. "You are the one to carry on our family name. And mark my word, you will walk on a far larger canvas than I."

Like his grandfather, Jack spent time among the people, getting to know them and their concerns. He rode subway cars and trains across town, shaking the hands of passengers and saying with a smile, "Hi, I'm Jack Kennedy." He marched in parades all over the city, greeting people on the sidelines. The Kennedy clan put all of its energy behind Jack's campaign, hosting house parties and gatherings to give people a chance to connect with him. Rose Kennedy and her daughters hosted endless tea parties to win the female vote.

As a politician of the people, Jack emphasized links between his life and the lives of the citizens he hoped to represent in Congress. Once he spoke before a gathering of the Gold Star Mothers, knowing that every woman in the room had lost a son in the war. He took Rose with him, and, sensing the emotion in the room, said simply, "I think I know how you feel. My mother is a Gold Star Mother, too." He left that day with every woman's vote secured.

On November 5, 1946, Jack won the election by a landslide: He received 73 percent of the vote, one of the largest victories in congressional history. Eighty-three-year-old Honey Fitz danced a jig on a table when the news came in.

As a rookie congressman, Jack spent a lot of time learning the process of the federal system. He studied the issues before him and voted to the best of his knowledge. In one controversial bill, he voted for educational funds to be used for the benefit of parochial as well as public schools. That vote drew even more attention to the fact that he was one of the few Catholics in Congress.

He voted in favor of labor unions when he denounced the Taft–Hartley Act (also known as the Labor–Management Relations Act of 1947), an attempt to reduce the power and effectiveness of the unions and therefore of the average working American. He also supported legislation that helped secure low-cost housing for those who couldn't afford it.

Although Jack was reelected to the House of Representatives two more times, in 1948 and 1950, he was setting his sights even higher.

THE KENNEDY CURSE

In August 1947, Jack visited Ireland to see Kathleen, his younger sister, who had always been a good friend and companion. Nicknamed "Kick" for her continually high spirits, she had moved to Ireland after her husband died during World War II. During his trip, Jack used a letter from an elderly aunt that outlined directions to the rural family home—a small house with a thatched roof—of family members he'd never met. Unlike their American

Jack was very close to his sister Kathleen, known affectionately as "Kick." Kathleen died on May 15, 1948, in a plane crash in France. The many deaths in his family began to affect Jack, who wondered if he, too, would die young.

relatives, the Irish Kennedys lived an impoverished life. Jack offered them money and asked how he could help, but all they asked was that he give the children a ride in his car.

Next, he traveled to London, where he became ill and was hurried to a hospital. Doctors diagnosed him with Addison's disease, which reduces the ability of the adrenal glands to produce cortisol, a hormone that helps the body handle stress. A lack of cortisol usually results in fatigue, weight loss, and weakness of the muscles. It also causes a person's skin to darken; Jack was known for his healthy tan, especially throughout his presidency, but historians now suspect it was a result of low cortisol levels. Jack's struggle with Addison's disease would last throughout his life. He regularly took medicine to keep his muscles strong—especially his back muscles, which were already weakened by his spine irregularity.

On May 15, 1948, after Jack had recovered from his bout with Addison's, the Kennedys received more bad news: Kick had died in a plane crash in France. Jack was stricken with grief over the death of another sibling, one who was a genuinely good friend. He started thinking obsessively about how death had struck down Joe Jr., Kick, and others in their prime. Given his many illnesses, he wondered, for the first time, if he would also die young.

> *"We must use time as a tool, not as a couch."*
>
> — John F. Kennedy, quoted in London's *The Observer* on December 10, 1961

SENATOR KENNEDY

On October 2, 1950, Honey Fitz died of a heart attack in Boston. It was yet another blow to the family. Remembering his grandfather's words of encouragement, Jack decided that he would begin walking on his "larger canvas." In January of 1951, he began his third term as congressman for the Eleventh District and, in April of 1952, he announced that he would run for a seat in the U.S. Senate for the state of Massachusetts.

His opponent in the race was Henry Cabot Lodge Jr., a veteran senator whose father had been a sworn political enemy of Honey Fitz. This only made Jack more determined to win, and he campaigned harder than he ever had in his life despite frequent attacks of Addison's disease and increasing back pain.

Once again, he relied on his family to help him succeed. His younger brother Bobby, a 26-year-old lawyer, agreed to serve as his campaign manager. His mother and sisters held the same tea parties that had proven so successful in his campaign for the House of Representatives. They hosted 35 such parties, which were attended by more than 50,000 women.

> *"We stand today on the edge of a new frontier—the frontier of the 1960s—a frontier of unknown opportunities and perils—a frontier of unfulfilled hopes and threats."*
>
> — John F. Kennedy, accepting the Democratic presidential nomination, July 15, 1960

Jack defeated Lodge on November 4, 1952, by a margin of more than 70,000 votes. Now, the Kennedys agreed, he was in a position to make a serious bid for

Roman Catholic Church in Newport, Rhode Island, and 1,200 attended the reception. It was the wedding of the decade. Jack was 36 and Jackie was 24.

THE SENATE YEARS

During his time in the Senate, Jack was faced with two major issues. The first was the severity of racism in the nation: The lynching of African Americans was commonplace, and segregation—the system of separating black and white Americans in education and public life—was being challenged. In May 1954, the Supreme Court of the United States ruled that racial segregation of public schools was unconstitutional. The case known as *Brown v. Board of Education of Topeka, Kansas* led to the integration of schools, which would allow schoolchildren of any race to attend schools based on the districts they lived in and not on the color of their skin. Jack consistently denounced racism and prejudice, perhaps because as a Catholic, he understood the unfairness of prejudice.

The other major issue was the "Red Scare." "Red" was a popular term for the Soviet Union and for communism in general. After World War II, the Soviet Union had emerged as a superpower threatening the United States. The following years were a period of tension known as the cold war. The early 1950s were a time in which any Americans suspected of sympathizing with communist ideals were rooted out and their careers ruined.

Wisconsin senator Joseph McCarthy led the attack. In February of 1950, McCarthy addressed a crowd in West Virginia. Waving a piece of paper in his hand, he proclaimed: "I have here in my hand a list of 205—a list of names that were made known to the secretary of state as being members of the Communist Party and who nevertheless are still working and shaping policy in the State Department." That speech grabbed national attention, and the lives of many people—artists, politicians, actors, and others—were shattered by the usually false and rarely supported accusations. "McCarthyism" sparked paranoia, making friends, neighbors, and colleagues suspicious of each other.

Though the cold war still raged, the Senate sought to censure, or formally condemn, Senator McCarthy's irresponsible behavior. On December 2, 1954, a monumental vote was held in the Senate chambers to issue disapproval of McCarthy for exploiting the fears of the American people. The motion passed by a vote of 67 to 22.

One senator was conspicuously absent that day and never voted.

COURAGE AND DEFEAT

With his back problems growing more severe, Jack relied more and more on crutches, though he made sure the media never saw them. In October of 1954, he underwent spinal surgery at the Hospital for Special Surgery in New York. He recuperated at the family home in Palm Beach, but underwent a second major surgery in February 1955.

Jack had health problems throughout his life. In the 1950s, back problems forced him to use crutches, which he tried to hide from the media. In 1954 and 1955, he underwent two major spinal surgeries. Recovery kept him away from Congress for seven months. He missed several important votes, including the McCarthy censure vote, which caused suspicion.

He would not recover sufficiently to return to work at the Senate until May, spending nearly seven months away from his congressional duties.

Jack's surgery caused him to miss the McCarthy censure vote in Congress. Because McCarthy was a close friend of the Kennedy family (he had been an usher in Bobby's wedding and had dated Eunice—another sister—for some time), many of his Senate colleagues did not see it that way. They thought Jack had avoided voting against a friend, that he had backed down from a true test of courage.

Jack was troubled by the implications. While resting at Palm Beach, he thought long and hard about what "courage" meant. McCarthy had certainly disgraced the Senate, but Jack knew that many senators in the past had defended their ideals, even risking unpopularity to do so.

He began working on a book about those senators, the little-known heroes of the government. Jackie helped him research it, making the countless trips to the library that Jack's weakened state prevented. When the book, *Profiles in Courage*, was published in January 1956, the dedication read "To my wife." It quickly became a bestseller.

> *"A man does what he must—in spite of personal consequences, in spite of obstacles and dangers and pressures—and that is the basis of all human morality."*
>
> — John F. Kennedy, *Profiles In Courage*

During his illness, Jack also spent time thinking about running for the presidency. At the Democratic

National Convention in August 1956, the young senator attempted to win the nomination for vice president. Adlai Stevenson, a seasoned Democratic politician, had secured the presidential nomination but could not decide between Jack Kennedy and Estes Kefauver for his running mate. Instead, he allowed the convention attendees to decide in a vote. Jack campaigned hard to win the nomination, spending all his time speaking to his colleagues and convincing them that he was the best choice. He barely saw Jackie, who was eight months pregnant, that entire weekend. In the end, his hard work did not pay off—he lost the nomination to Kefauver.

Disappointed, Jack flew to France with several friends to vacation away his sorrows. Even more bad news awaited him: On August 23, Jackie gave birth prematurely to a daughter, Arabella, who did not survive. Saddened, Jack immersed himself for the next year in his Senate work, serving on the Senate Labor Rackets Committee (formally known as the Senate Select Committee to Investigate Improper Activities in the Labor–Management Field). Despite his disappointment at losing the vice presidential nomination, he traveled around the country speaking in support of Stevenson and Kefauver. Though they lost the November 1956 election to Dwight Eisenhower and Richard Nixon, Jack's efforts earned him the favor and high regard of his colleagues in the Democratic Party. In January 1957, he was assigned to serve on the Senate Foreign Relations

Jack, pictured here signing autographs, won a Pulitzer Prize for his book *Profiles in Courage,* which detailed the actions of six Congressmen who fought for their often unpopular ideals. Jack's reflections on courage and ideals—a result of suspicions over the McCarthy vote—inspired the prize-winning book.

Committee, a position he had sought since first becoming a senator: Foreign policy had always been his interest, much more so than domestic issues.

Things improved for the Kennedys. Jackie became

pregnant again, and they again prepared to become parents. Then, in May 1957, Jack learned that *Profiles in Courage*, the book he had labored over while recovering from back surgery, had been awarded the Pulitzer Prize for biography or autobiography. Remembering that he had once told a reporter, "I would rather have the Pulitzer than be President," Jack began to think he might actually achieve both.

> *"The stories of past courage . . . can teach, they can offer hope, they can provide inspiration. But they cannot supply courage itself. For this each man must look into his own soul."*
>
> — **John F. Kennedy,** ***Profiles in Courage*****, 1956**

6

A Thousand Days

CAROLINE KENNEDY WAS born on November 27, 1957, to the great joy of her parents. Two years later, when Jack announced his candidacy for the presidency of the United States, his father purchased a small airplane for Jack to help him fly across the nation more easily and thus help with his campaigning. The proud new father dubbed the aircraft the *Caroline* for good luck.

Running for president presented several obstacles, including the fact that his opponent was Richard Nixon, the current vice president under Eisenhower. Jack's poor health was also a factor, although Jack masked his pain, allowing people to think he was in perfect physical health. Whenever he had to be hospitalized,

Jack and Jackie Kennedy are pictured on January 2, 1960, the day Jack announced his intention to run for president. His opponent was Richard Nixon, the current vice president of the United States. Jack's religion and his father's questionable political and business reputation were obstacles that he had to overcome in his campaign.

the press was told that his ailment was caused by old war injuries, thus reminding the public of his service in the war.

The other obstacle was his father's questionable reputation as a businessman and a politician. As the ambassador to Britain, Joseph Kennedy had not supported the United States' involvement in World War II and had gained enemies and friends alike in his business dealings. The public viewed him as a domineering man who wanted to control his children's political futures—which was not far from the truth.

Jack's religion was also an issue. America had never voted in a Catholic president, and irrational fears that Jack would be susceptible to the Vatican—and hold the pope's views above those of the American people—plagued Jack's campaign. A frustrated Jack told a friend, "Now I understand why Henry VIII set up his own church."

Nonetheless, Jack did well in the primaries, largely because of his strategy of appealing to the people's interests and concerns. At the Democratic National Convention in July of 1960, he was nominated as the Democratic Party's candidate; Lyndon Baines Johnson, an accomplished, experienced Texas senator, agreed to run as vice president.

Television—a relatively new medium—played a significant role in the 1960 presidential election: For the first time, people across the country could see the two candidates debating one another. In September and October 1960, Jack agreed to four televised debates with Nixon. The debates worked tremendously in his favor: Jack appeared youthful, tanned, and energetic, whereas Nixon came across as weary, wrinkled, and old.

In his speeches and campaign addresses, Jack hammered away at key points: He was a new candidate for a new generation of America. He targeted the young, postwar era citizens who wanted an enthusiastic leader to guide them through the Cold War, the fears of a Soviet attack, and the race crisis that was tearing the country apart.

> *"Let the word go forth from this time and place, to friend and foe alike, that the torch has been passed to a new generation of Americans. . . . Ask not what your country can do for you—ask what you can do for your country."*
>
> **— John F. Kennedy, presidential inaugural address, January 3, 1961**

The Kennedy clan again pitched in—even Jackie, media-shy and pregnant with their second child, campaigned for her husband. Indeed, her glamour, charm, and superstar quality played a pivotal role in helping portray Jack as a young, vigorous candidate who would revitalize the nation.

The night of the election, November 8, 1960, the race was head-to-head. As the votes rolled in and were counted, it was unclear who would win. In the early hours of the morning, an exhausted Jack finally concluded that the election would not be decided until the morning anyway, and he went to sleep.

The next morning, at 8:30 A.M., little Caroline rushed into her father's bedroom and jumped on his bed, pulling at the sheets. He woke up groaning but gave his daughter a kiss. Caroline then spoke the magic words her father was hoping to hear: "Good morning, Mr. President."

CAMELOT

Jack, now often referred to as "JFK," had made history in three ways: At 43, he was the youngest president elected (although not the youngest ever to serve as president: Vice President Teddy Roosevelt became president at age 42, when President William McKinley was assassinated); he was the first Catholic American president; and he had won the election by one of the most narrow margins in presidential history: 34,227,096 votes to Nixon's 34,108,546. That translated into 303 electoral votes for Jack versus Nixon's 219.

He soon had another reason to be elated: Jackie gave birth to their son, John Fitzgerald Kennedy Jr., a few weeks later, on November 25, 1960. The baby's first Christmas was spent with the family at Palm Beach, where Jack worked diligently on his inaugural address.

January 20, 1961, was a bitterly cold day in Washington, D.C. Despite the weather, the presidential inauguration was done Kennedy-style. Cardinal Richard Cushing, who had married Jack and Jackie, delivered the invocation shortly after noon. African-American opera singer Marian Anderson sang the national anthem—a sign, perhaps, of a president with a new perspective on race relations. Robert Frost, the New England poet whose verse had awed Jack as a young man, stood to read a poem he had composed especially for the occasion. The sharp wind, however, unsettled his papers, and the sun glare blinded

Jack was inaugurated as the 35th president of the United States on January 20, 1961. He was the youngest man and the only Catholic ever elected to the presidency and began the political era known as "Camelot," a time of glamour influenced by television and by the popular image of the Kennedys.

him, so he resorted to delivering "The Gift Outright," a poem he had committed to memory.

Then, at 12:51 P.M., Jack was sworn in as the 35th president of the United States. He took his oath to serve the nation with his hand on the Bible of his grandfather,

Honey Fitz, and then stepped forward to deliver the inaugural address he had labored over at Palm Beach.

The moving words electrified the American people. A gratified Jack was ready for the White House.

The rate of visitors to the White House soared from a daily high of 8,074 in early April 1961 to 13,575 by the end of the same month. Americans flocked to see how the young Kennedy family—the handsome president, his glamorous wife, and their two adorable children—lived. The Kennedys became America's royalty, idols in every sense of the word and role models for the nation. For example, to ease his back pain, Jack preferred sitting in a rocking chair; suddenly, rocking chairs became popular among American families. American women stormed fashion and clothing stores to copy Jackie's sense of style. The Kennedys frequently invited actors, writers, and artists to the White House, which revived interest in culture across the nation.

The era of Camelot, as it was known, was propelled mainly by two factors: The first was that television and other media broadcast the Kennedys to the world. Jack's frequent press conferences, as well as the media coverage of the family picnicking in the Rose Garden and riding horses, won the favor of the American people. Jack was photographed frequently in the Oval Office working while his children frolicked around him. The family's life became so public that Jackie strove to protect her children from the eye of the intrusive media. Once a press member asked her what she fed the family's new German shepherd. "Reporters," she snapped in response.

Nevertheless, the second factor that propelled Camelot was undeniably Jackie Kennedy herself: She possessed all the glamour of a Hollywood movie star and attracted crowds wherever she went. During a trip to Paris, the French people became frenzied over the First Lady, considering her one of their own because of her French ancestral roots, her sense of fashion, and her flawless French language skills. Jack began his speech by jokingly introducing himself not as the president of the United States, but as "the man who accompanied Jackie Kennedy to Paris" and added, "I have enjoyed it."

CIVIL RIGHTS

With the inauguration over, Jack settled into the White House to start performing his duties. He quickly discovered that Congress was divided almost down the middle between liberals and conservatives, making it almost impossible for him to pass legislation he supported.

Nonetheless, Jack did succeed in several other aspects. He told Americans, "We choose to go to the moon in this decade" and

> *"This Nation has tossed its cap over the wall of space, and we have no choice but to follow it. Whatever the difficulties, they will be overcome. Whatever the hazards, they must be guarded against. . . . We will climb this wall with safety and with speed—and we shall then explore the wonders on the other side."*
>
> **— John F. Kennedy, remarks at the dedication of the Aerospace Medical Health Center, November 21, 1963**

strengthened the air and space program. He also created a "new kind of American missionary," launching the Peace Corps, one of his most enduring triumphs. The Peace Corps offered young Americans a chance to explore the world, witness its tragedies, and do something meaningful to change it. Helping economically disadvantaged countries was important to his mission: To achieve that goal, he also created the Agency for

PRESIDENT KENNEDY'S LEGACY

Civil Rights Legislation

On July 2, 1964, President Lyndon Johnson signed the comprehensive civil rights legislation, The Civil Rights Act, into law. Johnson had pushed it aggressively through the House of Representatives and the Senate, where southern Democrats had obstructed earlier attempts to restore civil rights to black Americans. Johnson made it clear that the passing of the Civil Rights Act—which ensures that no American can be denied public service or public accommodations on the basis of race—was because of the slain President Kennedy, who had championed it in the first place.

As Kennedy said, on June 11, 1963, "It ought to be possible, in short, for every American to enjoy the privileges of being American without regard to his race or his color. In short, every American ought to have the right to be treated as he would wish to be treated, as one would wish his children to be treated."

The Civil Rights Acts was passed in 1964, shortly after his death, and is one of the reasons America is closer than ever before to a racially equal society. Black Americans have a legal foundation on which to confront discrimination, and all Americans benefit from the fact that nobody should suffer the evils of racism. Furthermore, we are a more diverse nation that embraces differences today because of the landmark legislation that Kennedy had the courage to advocate.

The space program is one of Jack's enduring legacies. He told the American people that they would reach the moon in the 1960s. Here he discusses the space capsule *Friendship 7* with astronaut John Glenn (left).

International Development (USAID) to assist in economic aid to the Third World.

One issue that hounded Jack's presidency was the injustice of segregation, which made American democracy seem like a farce to the rest of the world. As a member of an Irish-American Catholic family that understood the meaning of discrimination, Jack sympathized with the demands of civil rights activists for long overdue equality under the law. Still, he remained cautious about taking too liberal a stance on this issue because of the bloc of conservatives in Congress who could use it to make his presidency difficult. Jack therefore treaded carefully. During his campaign, he had hinted that he would end segregation in government-funded housing, but he failed to act on it. Black Americans and civil rights leaders felt betrayed.

> *"One hundred years of delay have passed since President Lincoln freed the slaves, yet their heirs, their grandsons, are not fully free. They are not yet freed from the bonds of injustice. They are not yet freed from social and economic oppression. And this Nation, for all its hopes and all its boasts, will not be fully free until all its citizens are free."*
>
> — John F. Kennedy, radio and television address to the American people, June 11, 1963

The Reverend Dr. Martin Luther King Jr., the charismatic leader of the civil rights movement, led peace marches and delivered powerful speeches across the South, stirring up a sense of justice in some Americans and sparking violence and fury among others. Things came to a head in September of 1962, when James Meredith, a black college student, attempted to enroll at the University of Mississippi ("Ole Miss"). The governor of Mississippi refused to integrate the university because the state still upheld segregation, even though the Supreme Court had ruled it unconstitutional. Mobs of angry white citizens rioted in the streets, forcing Meredith and the marshals protecting him to seek shelter in a dormitory for the night.

Jack, moved by Meredith's plight and just cause but too timid to act rashly and further inflame the violence, finally sent in the National Guard—federal troops—to allow Meredith to enter the college. The use of the federal troops as a last resort was applauded by most Americans, who rightly thought that Jack had successfully resolved the "Ole Miss" crisis. In 1963, Meredith would become the first black graduate of the University of Mississippi.

Jack continued to support civil rights quietly. In 1963, he introduced landmark legislation that would ban discrimination against black Americans on many levels, including the rights to vote, to attend integrated schools, and to have equal consumer access to restaurants and hotels. That legislation would not be passed until after his death.

7

The Communist Threat

THE ISSUE OF civil rights was Jack's most difficult domestic concern. The foreign policy issue that marked his presidency was the constant conflict with the Soviet Union, led by Premier Nikita Khrushchev in the early 1960s. Khrushchev was an aggressive leader, seeking to influence countries in Eastern Europe and Southeast Asia. Ruling the Soviet Union with an iron fist, Khrushchev pushed it to become the world's strongest nation. This led him into several diplomatic confrontations with the United States and its new, young president. Known as "the cold war" because no actual fighting took place, the tension between the two nations was a result of their different

The 1960s were a time of domestic and foreign conflict. The Red Scare—a fear of infiltration by Soviet communism—was a fear shared by many Americans. Jack met with Soviet Premier Nikita Khrushchev (left) in Vienna in June 1961 to discuss the future of Germany, at the time divided into communist and capitalist halves.

systems of government: communism versus democracy. These confrontations eventually threatened the well-being of the entire world, especially because both the United States and the Soviet Union possessed and were developing nuclear weapons.

Cuba, a small island nation off the coast of Florida,

soon came under the influence of Fidel Castro, a young Marxist who helped overthrow the corrupt government and seized power in 1959. Castro's sympathies clearly lay with communism and the Soviets. Nervous that a communist nation lay so close to America's borders, the American government under President Eisenhower drafted a plan to invade Cuba and oust Castro. It could not be known that the United States was behind the plan because that would be interpreted as an attack on a Soviet ally. Therefore, the United States recruited, trained, and armed 1,500 Cuban exiles to invade; the plan was that other Cubans, once they heard the news of the invasion, would help oust Castro.

Jack had just taken office when the time was deemed right for the invasion. Uncertain about following through with plans that another administration had drafted, Jack reluctantly approved it. On April 17, 1961, the band of exiles landed on the Bay of Pigs along Cuba's southern coast, waiting for American aircraft to back up their attempt. There had been some confusion, however, and the Americans never arrived. The exiles were captured, Cuban citizens in Havana were cordoned (surrounded by police) to prevent a revolution, and Castro remained a powerful figure who had now successfully thwarted an American-backed attack on his borders. The general consensus was that the Bay of Pigs incident was a ridiculous error in strategy and coordination on the part of the American military. Embarrassed by the blunder, Jack assumed full responsibility for this bleak beginning to his presidency.

DIVIDING A CITY

The Bay of Pigs would certainly not be Jack's last encounter—direct or indirect—with the Soviet Union. In June 1961, he met with Khrushchev in Vienna, Austria. This would be one of the most important meetings of his presidency. The two leaders discussed the future of Germany and its capital city Berlin: East Germany had adopted a communist government, but many citizens were fleeing to West Germany, where democracy and a capitalist system offered more opportunities. Berlin itself was divided into opposite halves. Kennedy and Khrushchev disagreed about the future of the city, and the talks failed to reach a resolution. By the end of that summer, the Soviets had erected a wall between the two halves of Berlin to prevent East Berliners from escaping.

The Berlin Wall became the ultimate symbol of communism's threat, and when he returned to the city in the summer of 1963, Jack told a large gathering that he hoped the wall would be one day brought down and Berlin's citizens reunited. Here he made his famous speech in which he meant to proclaim, "*Ich bin Berliner*" ("I am a citizen of Berlin"); instead, he said, "*Ich bin ein Berliner*" ("I am a jelly donut"). Despite the mistake, the enthusiastic crowd knew that the debonair, charismatic American president was expressing his solidarity with them.

THE CUBAN MISSILE CRISIS

The cold war was soon fought again on the diplomatic battlefield of Cuba, where Fidel Castro was still in power.

At 11:45 A.M. on October 16, 1962, Jack called an emergency session of his closest advisors, including his brother Bobby, now attorney general of the United States. These 14 men would be known as "ExComm," the Executive Committee of the National Security Council.

The news they heard that autumn morning was grim.

The night before, American reconnaissance planes had photographed Soviet nuclear missile sites being constructed in Cuba. The fact that the Soviet Union was installing nuclear weapons so close to the American border posed a direct threat to the safety of all Americans. A swift and sure response from the Kennedy administration was needed immediately.

The secretary of defense, Robert McNamara, cautioned against invading Cuba to dismantle the missiles—such an attack could prompt a nuclear war with the Soviets. Still, it remained an option, one to be followed only if all other measures failed. In the meantime, Jack opted for another of McNamara's suggestions, which was a more careful approach: to impose a quarantine, or blockade—around Cuba to prevent Soviet ships from reaching the island with more missile-building supplies. The Soviets criticized Kennedy, insisting that the missiles were there for defensive

> *"My fellow Americans, let us take that first step. Let us . . . step back from the shadow of war and seek out the way of peace. And if that journey is a thousand miles, or even more, let history record that we in this land at this time, took the first step."*
>
> **— John F. Kennedy, radio and television address to the American people on Nuclear Test Ban Treaty, July 26, 1963**

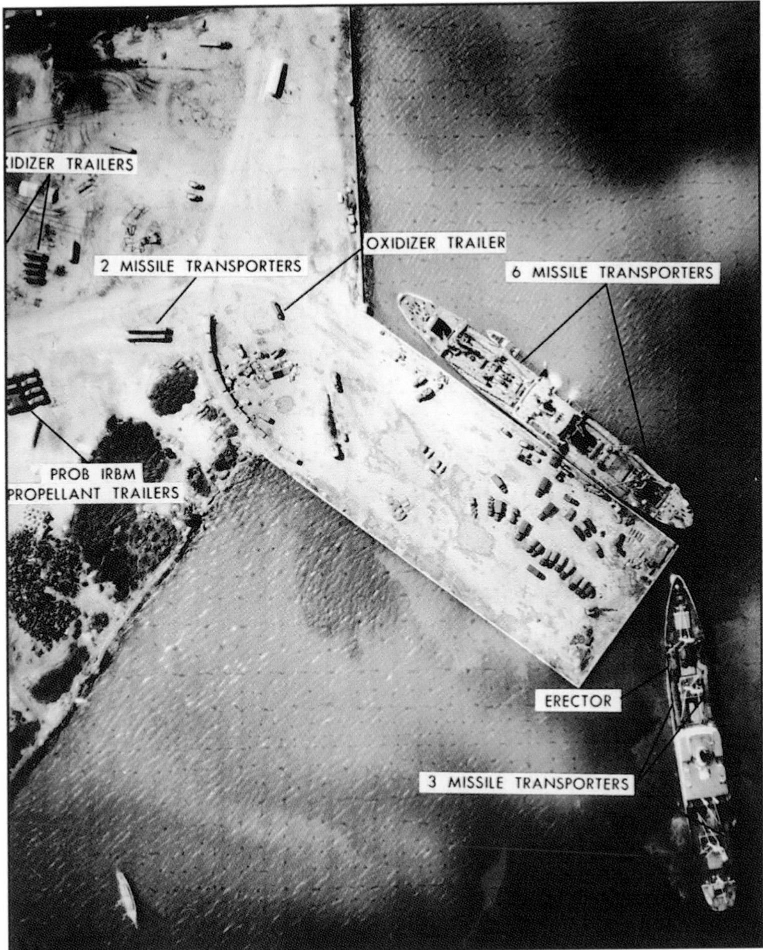

This 1962 U.S. Department of Defense photo shows Soviet missile equipment being loaded at a port in Cuba. This prompted Jack to proclaim a blockade around Cuba to prevent further nuclear weapons from arriving in the country. Soviet ships came closer, and tension in the United States mounted as the threat of nuclear war increased. This time is known as the Cuban Missile Crisis.

purposes only and not meant as part of a planned attack on the United States.

At 7:00 P.M. on October 22, Americans tuned their

television sets and radios to the president's address. Jack briefed the nation on the danger ahead and informed them that the quarantine around Cuba was in effect. He added, in a special message to Khrushchev, that the United States would "regard any nuclear missile launched from Cuba against any nation in the Western Hemisphere as an attack by the Soviet Union on the United States, requiring a full retaliatory response against the Soviet Union."

The Soviet ships headed toward Cuba seemed unwilling to stop. Khrushchev had plainly said that he regarded the quarantine as an act of war and intended to ignore it. The American ships that enforced the blockade, however, had orders to shoot at Soviet ships that tried to cross the blockade line. Everyone knew that war would erupt if either country's ships fired on the other.

Tension rose in the White House and across America as minute-by-minute reports came in to the president and ExComm about the status of Soviet vessels. Jack commented to his brother, "It looks really mean, doesn't it?" Indeed, across the nation, people prepared for nuclear war as best as they knew how—practicing techniques for seeking shelter from attack (which were actually ineffective) and emptying grocery store shelves of all canned and boxed foods.

The Soviet ships sailed closer and closer to the quarantine lines. Then, at approximately 10:30 A.M. on October 24, they stopped "dead in the water," according to the intelligence report. The Soviets had decided not to break the quarantine and risk war after all. Dean Rusk, the secretary of state, said in relief, "We're eyeball to eyeball and I think the other fellow just blinked."

On October 28, after an American reconnaissance pilot was shot down over Cuba and Bobby had held private meetings with the Soviet ambassador, an agreement to end the crisis was reached. The Soviets agreed to withdraw their missiles if the United States pledged not to

PRESIDENT KENNEDY'S LEGACY

Nuclear Test Ban Treaty

On July 25, 1963, the Limited Test Ban Treaty was signed by the United States, the Soviet Union, and Great Britain. It was a landmark treaty because it banned test explosions of nuclear weapons in outer space, underwater, and in the atmosphere. It clearly resulted from the fact that the two nations had come very close to nuclear war during the Cuban Missile Crisis of 1962; the world had waited tensely for 13 days to find out whether or not the actions of Kennedy and Premier Khrushchev would result in the destruction of life as they knew it.

Kennedy understood that the world could not afford to come that close to nuclear war again, so he pushed for agreement between the nations on such a treaty. Neither country totally trusted the other, but Kennedy knew that one value they shared was upholding the security of people around the world. In his address at American University on a Comprehensive Nuclear Test Ban, he said, "Among the many traits the peoples of our two countries have in common, none is stronger than our mutual abhorrence of war. Almost unique among the major world powers, we have never been at war with each other."

Indeed, Kennedy's ability to think carefully through such a dire situation and reflect on its meaning for all of humanity has influenced other world leaders as well. Although countries continue to develop nuclear weapons, the world has not seen the use of them in war since World War II.

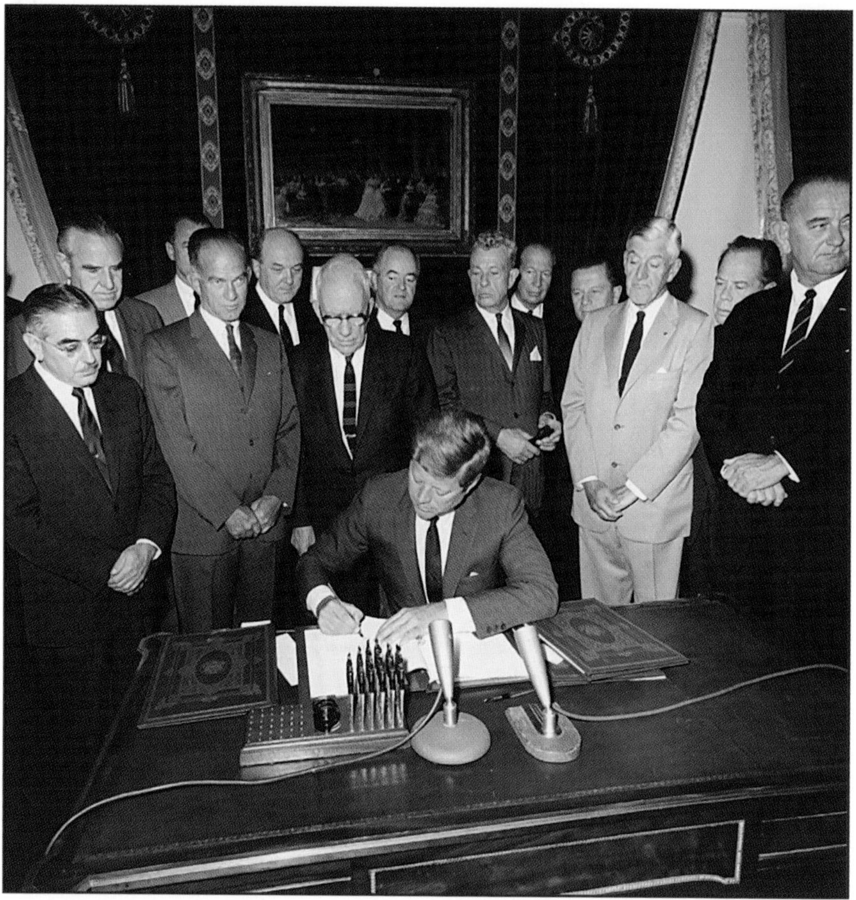

Nuclear war was narrowly averted in the Cuban Missile Crisis. Jack wanted to ensure that it could not happen again and proposed a treaty banning the testing of nuclear weapons. He signed the Nuclear Test Ban Treaty on October 7, 1963, while surrounded by his advisors and Vice President Lyndon Johnson (far right).

invade Cuba. The Cuban Missile Crisis, the 13 most difficult days in Jack's presidency and his life, was safely over, thanks largely to his calm in the midst of a terrifying storm.

With his usual foresight, Jack wanted to ensure that the

world never again faced such a disaster. On July 26, 1963, he addressed the nation about a nuclear test ban treaty he had initiated and which had been signed by the world's most powerful nations: "This limited treaty will radically reduce the nuclear testing which would otherwise be conducted on both sides; it will prohibit the United States, the United Kingdom, the Soviet Union, and all others who sign it, from engaging in the atmospheric tests which have so alarmed mankind; and it offers to all the world a welcome sign of hope."

> *"Today every inhabitant of this planet must contemplate that day when this planet may no longer be habitable. Every man, woman and child lives under a nuclear sword of Damocles, hanging by the slenderest of threads, capable of being cut at any moment by accident or miscalculation or madness. The weapons of war must be abolished before they abolish us."*
>
> **— John F. Kennedy, address to the United Nations General Assembly, September 25, 1961**

Assassination and Aftermath

BY THE SUMMER of 1963, Jackie was pregnant again, and the joyous parents—and the nation—waited to hear about the first child that would be born in the White House. On August 7, Patrick Bouvier Kennedy was born six weeks premature. The second son of the president and First Lady struggled to survive but suffered from respiratory problems. He died two days later.

Jackie was inconsolable, as was Jack. He had suffered terribly during the deaths of his brother Joe Jr. and his sister Kathleen, but he grieved over the loss of his own child as he had not grieved for anyone else. "He put up quite a fight," Jack wept. "He was a beautiful baby."

Jack and Jackie had two surviving children: Caroline (far right) and John Jr. (second from left). Jack and Jackie were heartbroken that their two other children, Arabella, the firstborn, and Patrick, the last, did not survive infancy.

One day, a distraught Caroline brought her dead canary into the Oval Office. She planned to bury it in the Rose Garden but wanted to show it first to her father, who sat at his desk. When she held the lifeless bird up to him, he jumped back, startled, and yelled, "Get it away!"

Death seemed to be in the air.

THE DEATH OF CAMELOT

Jackie Kennedy didn't want to go to Texas. Neither did the president. Jackie was weary of the media, of being paraded before crowds of people, and longed for her privacy. Jack had a different reason: He needed to win the votes of Texans to be reelected, but he had barely carried the state in 1960. A very conservative state, Texas did not typically agree with Kennedy's liberal policies. If he were going to win the 1964 election, he had to reach out to the people of Texas.

Part of the trip, planned for November 22, 1963, included a motorcade drive through the streets of Dallas. The drive began shortly before noon. Governor John Connally and his wife sat in the limousine with Jack and Jackie as the convertible, with its top down, wound its way through the streets at ten miles per hour. The crowds lining the streets to see their president applauded wildly, making Jack feel more confident and welcome in the conservative state. Mrs. Connally turned to the president and said, "Mr. President, you can't say Dallas doesn't love you."

At 12:30 P.M., as the limousine crawled past the Texas School Book Depository, a shot rang out. The bullet pierced the president's neck, entering from the back and exiting from the front of his throat. "My God, I am hit!" he cried out, clutching his throat. Jackie, who had been waving to the crowds, turned to him just as another rifle shot cracked through the air.

The president could have survived the first wound,

Jack needed to win votes in Texas in order to be reelected to the presidency, so he and Jackie planned a trip to that state. Part of their trip included a motorcade through the streets of Dallas with the governor and his wife. Jack was fatally shot in the head as the car moved slowly down the street. Although some uncertainty remains, the prevailing theory is that Lee Harvey Oswald, a Cuban sympathizer, was the lone gunman.

but the second bullet was fatal, shattering the right side of his skull. He collapsed, and Jackie cradled his body, screaming, "Oh, my God, they have shot my husband. I love you, Jack."

Secret Service agents raced to nearby Parkland Memorial Hospital, where doctors pronounced the president dead at 1:00 P.M. Vice President Johnson, with a stunned Jackie beside him, was sworn in as the 36th president of the United States aboard Air Force One, the presidential plane that carried Jack's body back to Washington, D.C.

> *"The courage of life is often a less dramatic spectacle than the courage of a final moment; but it is no less than a magnificent mixture of triumph and tragedy."*
>
> — John F. Kennedy
> *Profiles In Courage*

The bullets had been fired from the rifle of Lee Harvey Oswald, a Cuban sympathizer who crouched behind a window on the upper floor of the Texas School Book Depository. Two days later, Oswald would be killed by Jack Ruby, a nightclub owner. Many people suspected that Jack had been murdered as part of a conspiracy, so the Warren Commission was established by President Johnson to investigate the assassination. The commission concluded that Oswald had acted alone in the shooting of the president, though today there are still rumors and conspiracy theories that perhaps the Mafia and even the CIA played a role in the assasination.

THE LEGACY OF JFK

Like Joe Jr., Kathleen, and his childhood hero, Lord Byron, Jack died young, killed in his prime. What Oswald's bullets never could have wounded was Jack's enduring legacy. As president for a new generation of Americans, he led the

One of the most enduring images of the end of Camelot is this photograph of two and a half-year-old John Jr. saluting his father's casket.

nation with all the energy of his youth and all the wisdom of his predecessors.

Many of the programs he established, such as the Peace Corps, continue to thrive today and to inspire new generations of Americans to serve their country and the world. His landmark nuclear test ban treaties helped calm the storm of

PRESIDENT KENNEDY'S LEGACY

The Peace Corps

In his inaugural speech, John F. Kennedy challenged young Americans who wanted to make a difference to consider the world, not just the nation, as their mission. His words inspired millions: "To those people in the huts and villages across the globe struggling to break the bonds of mass misery, we pledge our best efforts to help them help themselves." On March 1, 1961, an executive order of the president established the Peace Corps, an organization that would allow young Americans the opportunity to volunteer in countries stricken with poverty and war.

Kennedy appointed Sargent Shriver as its first director, and soon assignments had been created to send American volunteers to Ghana, Tanzania, Colombia, the Philippines, Chile, and St. Lucia. More than 5,000 applicants took the first exams to enter the Peace Corps.

By 1966, 15,000 volunteers were working in different countries, promoting a better understanding of Americans among peoples of those nations, as well as an understanding of other nations and cultures among Americans. By 1974, Peace Corps volunteers were stationed in 67 different countries around the globe; by 1981, the twentieth anniversary of its establishment, that number had risen to 88 countries. The fact that the cold war marred much of Kennedy's presidency gives special emphasis to the fact that in 1992, volunteers were assigned to the former Soviet Union to promote peace and fellowship. The Peace Corps is one of Kennedy's most enduring legacies—it is an agency that continues to inspire generations of young Americans to reach out to the world.

the cold war. The civil rights legislation he introduced in Congress was passed shortly after his death.

> *"In the decade that lies ahead—in the challenging revolutionary sixties—the American Presidency will demand . . . that the President place himself in the very thick of the fight, that he care passionately about the fate of the people he leads, that he be willing to serve them, at the risk of incurring their momentary displeasure."*
>
> — John F. Kennedy, "The Presidency in 1960," speech, January 14, 1960

With his eyes simultaneously on the past, present, and future, Jack's actions paralleled his belief in the love of mankind. He envisioned a nation and a world united in, rather than divided by, its common interests. As he eloquently said, "In the final analysis, our most basic common link is that we all inhabit this small planet, we all breathe the same air, we all cherish our children's futures, and we are all mortal."

THE PRESIDENTS OF THE UNITED STATES

George Washington
1789–1797

John Adams
1797–1801

Thomas Jefferson
1801–1809

James Madison
1809–1817

James Monroe
1817–1825

John Quincy Adams
1825–1829

Andrew Jackson
1829–1837

Martin Van Buren
1837–1841

William Henry Harrison
1841

John Tyler
1841–1845

James Polk
1845–1849

Zachary Taylor
1849–1850

Millard Filmore
1850–1853

Franklin Pierce
1853–1857

James Buchanan
1857–1861

Abraham Lincoln
1861–1865

Andrew Johnson
1865–1869

Ulysses S. Grant
1869–1877

Rutherford B. Hayes
1877–1881

James Garfield
1881

Chester Arthur
1881–1885

Grover Cleveland
1885–1889

Benjamin Harrison
1889–1893

Grover Cleveland
1893-1897

William McKinley
1897–1901

Theodore Roosevelt
1901–1909

William H. Taft
1909–1913

Woodrow Wilson
1913–1921

Warren Harding
1921–1923

Calvin Coolidge
1923–1929

Herbert Hoover
1929–1933

Franklin D. Roosevelt 1933–1945

Harry S. Truman
1945–1953

Dwight Eisenhower
1953–1961

John F. Kennedy
1961–1963

Lyndon Johnson
1963–1969

Richard Nixon
1969–1974

Gerald Ford
1974–1977

Jimmy Carter
1977–1981

Ronald Reagan
1981–1989

George H.W. Bush
1989–1993

William J. Clinton
1993–2001

George W. Bush
2001–

Note: Dates indicate years of presidential service.
Source: www.whitehouse.gov

Presidential Fact File

THE CONSTITUTION

Article II of the Constitution of the United States outlines several requirements for the president of the United States, including:

- ★ **Age:** The president must be at least 35 years old.
- ★ **Citizenship:** The president must be a U.S. citizen.
- ★ **Residency:** The president must have lived in the United States for at least 14 years.
- ★ **Oath of Office:** On his inauguration, the president takes this oath: "I do solemnly swear (or affirm) that I will faithfully execute the office of President of the United States, and will to the best of my ability, preserve, protect and defend the Constitution of the United States."
- ★ **Term:** A presidential term lasts four years.

PRESIDENTIAL POWERS

The president has many distinct powers as outlined in and interpreted from the Constitution. The president:

- ★ Submits many proposals to Congress for regulatory, social, and economic reforms.
- ★ Appoints federal judges with the Senate's approval.
- ★ Prepares treaties with foreign nations to be approved by the Senate.
- ★ Can veto laws passed by Congress.
- ★ Acts as commander in chief of the military to oversee military strategy and actions.
- ★ Appoints members of the cabinet and many other agencies and administrations with the Senate's approval.
- ★ Can declare martial law (control of local governments within the country) in times of national crisis.

TRADITION

Many parts of the presidency developed out of tradition. The traditions listed below are but a few that are associated with the U.S. presidency.

- ★ After taking his oath of office, George Washington added, "So help me God." Numerous presidents since Washington have also added this phrase to their oath.
- ★ Originally, the Constitution limited the term of the presidency to four years, but did not limit the number of terms a president could serve. Presidents, following the precedent set by George Washington, traditionally served only two terms. After Franklin Roosevelt was elected to four terms, however, Congress amended the Constitution to restrict presidents to only two.
- ★ James Monroe was the first president to have his inauguration outside the Capitol. From his inauguration in 1817 to Jimmy Carter's inauguration in 1977, it was held on the Capitol's east portico. Ronald Reagan broke from this tradition in 1981 when he was inaugurated on the west portico to face his home state, California. Since 1981, all presidential inaugurations have been held on the west portico of the Capitol.
- ★ Not all presidential traditions are serious, however. One of the more fun activities connected with the presidency began when President William Howard Taft ceremoniously threw out the first pitch of the new baseball season in 1910. Presidents since Taft have carried on this tradition, including Woodrow Wilson, who is pictured here as he throws the first pitch of the 1916 season. In more recent years, the president has also opened the All-Star and World Series games.

Presidential Fact File

THE WHITE HOUSE

Although George Washington was involved with the planning of the White House, he never lived there. It has been, however, the official residence of every president beginning with John Adams, the second U.S. president. The building was completed approximately in 1800, although it has undergone several renovations since then. It was the first public building constructed in Washington, D.C. The White House has 132 rooms, several of which are open to the public. Private rooms include those for administration and the president's personal residence. For an online tour of the White House and other interesting facts, visit the official White House website, *http://www.whitehouse.gov.*

THE PRESIDENTIAL SEAL

A committee began planning the presidential seal in 1777. It was completed in 1782. The seal appears as an official stamp on medals, stationery, and documents, among other items. Originally, the eagle faced right toward the arrows (a symbol of war) that it held in its talons. In 1945, President Truman had the seal altered so that the eagle's head instead faced left toward the olive branch (a symbol of peace), because he believed the president should be prepared for war but always look toward peace.

President Kennedy in Profile

PERSONAL

Name: John Fitzgerald Kennedy

Birth date: May 29, 1917

Birth place: Brookline, Massachusetts

Father: Joseph Patrick Kennedy

Mother: Rose Elizabeth Fitzgerald

Wife: Jacqueline Bouvier

Children: Arabella, Caroline, John, and Patrick

Death date: November 22, 1963

Death place: Dallas, Texas

POLITICAL

Years in office: 1961–1963

Vice president: Lyndon Baines Johnson

Occupations before presidency: Author, public official

Political party: Democrat

Major achievements of presidency: Civil rights, space program

Nickname: JFK

Presidential library:

The John F. Kennedy Library and Museum
Columbia Point
Boston, MA 02125
(877) 616-4599
http://www. jfklibrary.org

Tributes:

The John F. Kennedy Center for the Performing Arts (Washington, D.C.; *http://www.kennedy-center.org/*)

Kennedy Space Center (Brevard County, Fla.; *http://www.ksc.nasa.gov/*)

John F. Kennedy National Historic Site (Brookline, Mass.; *http://www.nps.gov/jofi/*)

Chronology

1917 John Fitzgerald Kennedy is born in Brookline, Massachusetts, to Joseph and Rose Kennedy on May 29.

1931 Kennedy begins his freshman year at the Choate School.

1935 Kennedy graduates from Choate.

1936 After withdrawing from Princeton University because of illness, Kennedy begins studies a year late at Harvard University.

1939 World War II is declared on September 1.

1940 **June** Kennedy graduates cum laude from Harvard University.

August 1 Kennedy's thesis, which received a magna cum laude, is published as a book entitled *Why England Slept.*

1941 **October 8** Kennedy enlists in the Naval Reserve.

December 7 Japan attacks the U.S. naval base at Pearl Harbor, Hawaii; the next day, the United States enters World War II.

1943 *PT-109* is sunk by the Japanese destroyer, the *Amagiri* on August 2. Kennedy and his crew are stranded for several days in the South Pacific until they are rescued.

1944 Joseph Kennedy Jr. is killed while flying a bombing mission on August 12.

1945 Kennedy works as a reporter for the Hearst newspaper company between April and June.

1946 Kennedy is elected to the House of Representatives as a congressman for Massachusetts.

1948 Kathleen Kennedy, John Fitzegerald Kennedy's sister, is killed in an airplane crash in France.

1952 Kennedy is elected to the U.S. Senate after serving three terms as a congressman.

1953 Kennedy marries Jacqueline Lee Bouvier on September 12.

1956 **January 1** *Profiles in Courage,* which Kennedy wrote in 1955 while recovering from a major spinal surgery, is published.

August 23 The Kennedy's first child, Arabella, is born prematurely and dies.

1957 **May 6** *Profiles in Courage* wins the Pulitzer Prize, the nation's highest literary honor, in the category of biography or autobiography.

November 27 Jacqueline gives birth to Caroline Kennedy on Thanksgiving Day.

1958 Kennedy is reelected to U.S. Senate by a wide margin.

1960 **January 2** Kennedy announces his intentions to run for president of the United States.

July 13 Kennedy wins the Democratic Party nomination to run as its candidate in the 1960 presidential election; Lyndon Baines Johnson runs as the vice presidential candidate.

September 26 Kennedy and his opponent, Richard Nixon, participate in the first nationally televised presidential debate, the first in a series of four, all of which are considered victories for Kennedy.

November 8 Kennedy wins the election, becoming the 35th president of the United States and, at the age of 43, the youngest man ever elected to the office.

November 25 Jacqueline gives birth to John F. Kennedy Jr.

1961 **April 17** The Bay of Pigs invasion of Cuba fails disastrously.

June 3–4 Kennedy meets with Nikita Khrushchev, the Soviet premier, in Vienna.

September 22 Kennedy signs legislation establishing the Peace Corps.

1962 **September 30** Kennedy orders federal marshals to control the violence when James Meredith attempts to enroll at the University of Mississippi. In an address to the nation, he criticizes racially motivated attempts to prevent James Meredith from seeking an education.

October 16–28 The Cuban Missile Crisis, the greatest test of Kennedy's presidency, is resolved without war.

1963 **June 19** Kennedy submits a landmark bill, which will reform civil rights, to Congress.

July 25 Largely because of the efforts of Kennedy, the United States, the Soviet Union, and Great Britain sign a treaty to limit the testing of nuclear weapons.

August 11 Patrick Bouvier Kennedy, Jacqueline and John F. Kennedy's second son, dies only two days after his premature birth.

November 22 Kennedy is assassinated during a trip to Dallas, Texas, at the age of 46.

"Addison's Disease." National Institute of Diabetes and Digestive and Kidney Diseases. *http://www.niddk.nih.gov/health/endo/pubs/addison/addison.htm#causes.*

"The Cuban Missile Crisis." National Security Archives. *http://www.gwu.edu/~nsarchiv/nsa/cuba_mis_cri/621026_621115 %20Chronology%201.pdf.*

Harrison, Barbara, and Daniel Terris. *A Twilight Struggle: The Life of John Fitzgerald Kennedy*. New York: Lothrop, Lee & Shepard, 1992.

"Jacqueline Lee Bouvier Kennedy." White House Web site. *http://www.whitehouse.gov /history/firstladies/jk35.html.*

Kennedy, John F. "Commencement Address at American University." JFK Library Web site. *http://www.cs.umb.edu/jfklibrary/j061063.htm.*

Kennedy, John F. "Popular Quotations." JFK Library Web site. *http://www.cs.umb.edu/jfklibrary/jfkquote.htm.*

Kennedy, John F. "Speeches." JFK Library Web site. *http://www.cs.umb.edu/jfklibrary/speeches.htm.*

Kennedy, John F. "Radio And Television Address to the American People on the Nuclear Test Ban Treaty." JFK Library Web site. *http://www.cs.umb.edu/jfklibrary/j072663.htm.*

Parmet, Herbert S. *JFK: The Presidency of John F. Kennedy*. New York: Viking Press, 1984.

Perret, Geoffrey. *Jack: A Life Like No Other*. New York: Random House, 2001.

"Report of the President's Commission on the Assassination of President Kennedy." U.S. National Archives and Records Administration. *http://www.archives.gov/research_room/jfk/warren_commission/ warren_commission_report_chapter2.html#drive.*

Winston Churchill Center Web site. *http://www.winstonchurchill.org/acthour.htm*

Whitney, David C., and Robin Vaughn Whitney. *American Presidents.* New York: Simon and Schuster.

Further Reading

Abraham, Philip. *John F. Kennedy and PT109.* Chicago: Children's Press, 2002.

Cole, Michael D. *John F. Kennedy: President of the New Frontier.* Berkeley Heights, N.J.: Enslow Publishers, Inc., 1996.

Cooper, Ilene. *Jack: The Early Years of John F. Kennedy.* New York: Dutton Books, 2003.

Donnelly, Judy. *Who Shot the President?* New York: Random House, 1988.

Harrison, Barbara, and Daniel Terris. *A Twilight Struggle: The Life of John Fitzgerald Kennedy.* New York: Lothrop, Lee & Shepard, 1992.

Hossell, Karen Price. *The Assassination of John F. Kennedy: Death of the New Frontier.* Crystal Lake, Ill.: Heinemann Library, 2002.

Kennedy, John Fitzgerald. *Profiles in Courage.* New York: Harper, 1956.

———. *A Nation of Immigrants.* New York: Harper, 1964.

Lindop, Edmund. *Dwight D. Eisenhower, John F. Kennedy, Lyndon B. Johnson.* New York: Twenty-First Century Books, 1996.

Randall, Marta. *John F. Kennedy.* New York: Chelsea House, 1988.

Sandak, Cass R. *The Kennedys.* New York: Crestwood House, 1991.

Schoor, Gene. *Young John Kennedy.* New York: Harcourt, Brace & World, 1963.

Spencer, Lauren. *The Assassination of John F. Kennedy.* New York: Rosen Publishing Group, 2002.

Swisher, Clarice, ed. *John F. Kennedy.* San Diego, Cal.: Greenhaven Press, 2000.

Uschan, Michael V. *John F. Kennedy.* San Diego, Cal.: Lucent Books, 1999.

INDEX

INDEX

INDEX

Index

Picture Credits

page:

11: © CORBIS
15: Courtesy of the John Fitzgerald Kennedy Library, Boston
17: © Bachrach Photographers/Courtesy of the John Fitzgerald Kennedy Library, Boston
21: Courtesy of the John Fitzgerald Kennedy Library, Boston
26: © Bettmann/CORBIS
30: Courtesy of the John Fitzgerald Kennedy Library, Boston
33: Courtesy of the John Fitzgerald Kennedy Library, Boston
37: Courtesy of the John Fitzgerald Kennedy Library, Boston
40: Courtesy of the John Fitzgerald Kennedy Library, Boston
43: Courtesy of the John Fitzgerald Kennedy Library, Boston
46: © Bettmann/CORBIS
52: © Bettmann/CORBIS
55: © Bettmann/CORBIS
58: Courtesy of the John Fitzgerald Kennedy Library, Boston
61: © Bettmann/CORBIS
65: © Bettmann/CORBIS
69: © Associated Press, AP
73: © Associated Press, AP
77: © Associated Press, DEPARTMENT OF DEFENSE
80: Courtesy of the John Fitzgerald Kennedy Library, Boston
83: © Bettmann/CORBIS
85: © Bettmann/CORBIS
87: © Bettmann/CORBIS
90-91: Courtesy Library of Congress, "Portraits of the Presidents and First Ladies" American Memory Collection

Cover: John F. Kennedy Library, Columbia Point, Boston, MA

Acknowledgments

Thank you to Celebrity Speakers Intl. for coordinating Mr. Cronkite's contribution to this book.

Susan Muaddi Darraj (*http://www.SusanMuaddiDarraj.com*) is a freelance writer based in Baltimore, Maryland. She has authored numerous articles, short fiction, and books, and she also teaches college-level English and writing courses. She is currently working on other biographies and a collection of short fiction.

Walter Cronkite has covered virtually every major news event during his more than 60 years in journalism, during which he earned a reputation for being "the most trusted man in America." He began his career as a reporter for the United Press during World War II, taking part in the beachhead assaults of Normandy and covering the Nuremberg trials. He then joined *CBS News* in Washington, D.C., where he was the news anchor for political convention and election coverage from 1952 to 1980. CBS debuted its first half-hour weeknight news program with Mr. Cronkite's interview of President John F. Kennedy in 1963. Mr. Cronkite was inducted into the Academy of Television Arts and Sciences in 1985 and has written several books. He lives in New York City with his wife of 59 years.